IN
OTHER
WORDS

To Anthony
Love in Christ
Dot Kryh

IN
OTHER
WORDS

David Paul Garty

Library of Congress Control Number:		2021901893
ISBN:	Hardcover	978-1-6641-6764-3
	Softcover	978-1-6641-6763-6
	eBook	978-1-6641-6762-9

Print information available on the last page.

Rev. date: 04/06/2021

To order additional copies of this book, contact:
Xlibris
844-714-8691
www.Xlibris.com
Orders@Xlibris.com
827997

Contents

How many other words can you find within the title?

In Other Words

THE	THIN	THINE	THEN	THIS	THOSE
ORDER	DROWN	OWN	ROW	DOW	DOWN
HOW	NOW	HEWN	INTO	ONTO	ROD
RODE	RODEO	HOT	NOT	DOT	ROT
DOOR	HOOD	SOOT	SIN	SINE	SHIN
SHINE	SHINED	SWORD	RED	WORSE	WORSEN
THRONE	THROW	THROWN	NEW	DEW	DREW
RENT	HINT	HINTED	HINDER	DINT	DENT
SENT	WORE	HOOT	ROOT	TIRE	TIRED
DIRE	SIRE	SIREN	HORN	HORNET	WIRE
WINE	WHINE	WHINED	WREN	WIN	SON
HON	HONE	TONE	DONE	WOO	WHO
ERR	SHOT	SHOOT	SHORT	SHOOTER	SHORTER
SHORTEN	SHORTED	SORT	SORTED	REST	RINSE
RITE	RITED	ROSTER	ROSE	HOSE	HOSED
NOSE	WONDER	SOOTHE	REND	WON	DREW
DRONE	DOTH	WED	WENT	RODE	WOOD
WOODEN	TOO	TORE	STORE	STONE	STORED
STONED	HONOR	HONORED	SWORE	HER	HERO

Of course, this is not an exhaustive list. All the words found in other words have at least three letters. However, the words are in your hands now. Feel free to use two letter words and/or contractions if you would like.

My ten-year old niece and many of the residents who stay at the nursing home type facility where I work helped me search through all the words on the following pages. We wrote down all the words we could find within other words. But you may find many more. More than fifty words were found in each of the other words. Many times, one hundred or more words were found in other words contained within these pages. Expand the way you look at words, or better yet, help someone else expand their way of thinking. Either way, have fun trying. How many words can you find in other words on the following pages?

Misunderstanding

Exasperation

Fecilitation

Unidentified

Exacerbation

Organization

Malnutrition

Architecture

Appreciation

Communicator

Ressurection

Expectations

Ambidextrous

Compensation

Sporadically

Abbreviations

Acquaintance

Championship

Conversation

Relationship

Righteousness

Entertainment

Weightlifting

Concentration

Quadrilateral

Contemplating

Extraordinary

Encouragement

Revolutionary

Skateboarding

Determination

Enlightenment

Mathematician

Professionally

Photosynthesis

Neutralization

Accountability

Specialization

Administration

Understandable

Acknowledgement

Kindheartedness

Trustworthiness

Insubordination

Miniaturization

Anticoagulation

Extraterrestrial

Absentmindedness

Characterization

Multiprogramming

Anesthesiologist

Investigatory

Enthusiastically

Hydroelectricity

Undifferentiated

Apprehensiveness

Neurotransmitter

Responsibilities

Environmentalist

Creditworthiness

Overcompensation

Emotionalization

Administratively

Counterbalancing

Misappropriation

Contraindication

Hyperventilation

Disqualification

Broncopneumonia

Incomprehensible

Interdisciplinary

Industrialization

Decriminalization

Telecommunication

Misrepresentation

Spondylolisthesis

Misinterpretation

Brokenheartedness

Tenderheartedness

Characteristically

Territorialization

Unappreciativeness

Hydroxychloroquine

Straightforwardness

Sternocleidomastoid

Conventionalization

Individualistically

Compartmentalization

Extravaganzas

Combustion

Gingerbread

Superintendent

Decorations

Togetherness

Poinsettia

Justification

Subsequential

Constitutionality

Intentionally

Significantly

Safeguarding

Internalizing

Factualizing

Affectionately

Configuration

Capitalization

Supplementary

Slaughterhouse

Sledgehammer

Descriptively

Weightbearing

Comfortableness

Butterscotch

Brainstorming

Journalistically

Inumerable

Indiscriminately

Frontiersman

Kaleidoscope

Juxtapositional

Kleptomaniac

Knowledgeable

Sympathizing

Unbeknownst

Ventriloquism

Intellectualism

Aerodynamically

Accomplishments

Allegorizations

Anthropologists

Argumentatively

Beautifications

Biomechanically

Bronchodilators

Circumscription

Condescendingly

Consequentially

Counterproductive

Uncompromisable

Decontaminating

Troubleshooters

Defibrillations

Subcategorizing

Fingerprintings

Redistributions

Demographically

Quadruplicating

_____

_____

_____

_____

_____

_____

_____

_____

_____

_____

_____

_____

_____

_____

_____

_____

_____

_____

_____

_____

_____

_____

_____

_____

_____

_____

_____

_____

_____

Counterproposal

Squeezabilities

Discombobulated

Diversification

More Words

PERPENDICULARLY	GENERALIZATIONS	OVEREMPHASIZING
HALLUCINOGENICS	OUTDOORSMANSHIP	IMPROVISATIONAL
NEARSIGHTEDNESS	INDIVIDUALISTIC	MANEUVERABILITY
JURISPRUDENTIAL	LACKADAISICALLY	KINDERGARTENERS
KINESTHETICALLY	INTERJECTIONS	SIMULTANEOUSLY
LUMBERJACKING	CONTEMPORANEOUSLY	PREACCOMODATIONS
UNCONDITIONALLY	FRANKFURTERS	IMPOSSIBILITIES
INVESTIGATION	CANTANKEROUS	EXHILARATING
REFRIGERATOR	INVESTIGATIVELY	ENCYCLOPEDIA
METEOROLOGISTS	NEIGHBORHOODS	HEADQUARTERS
REPRODUCTION	APPROACHABLE	OVERWHELMING
REABSORPTION	CANCELLATIONS	CARBOHYDRATES
CONQUISTADOR	CHOREOGRAPHY	INTOXICATING
PROTUBERANCE	OVERACHIEVERS	BREATHTAKING
FAITHFULNESS	REJUVENATION	EQUIVOCATING
ASPHYXIATION	AMPHITHEATER	SUBCUTANEOUS
PEACEKEEPING	INCOMPARABLE	DISINTEGRATED
ADEQUATENESS	INDISTINGUISHABLE	UNIMAGINABLE
AUTHENTICATING	UNDEFEATABLE	ILLUSTRATIVELY
UNAPPROPRIATED	GRACIOUSNESS	NONCOLLAPSIBLE
UNCOMPROMISINGLY	ALPHABETICALLY	PREREQUISITE
COMPATABILITY	EXUBERANTLY	ACQUAINTANCES
APPOINTMENTS	PROGNOSTICATION	APPLEFRITTERS
PRECAUTIONARY	REQUIREMENTS	VALENTINE'S DAY

In my search for more words, greater than 40,000 words were found having twelve or more letters. The residents at the nursing home and I have used our own names and the names of former Presidents of the United States. There may be endless possibilities from which to draw words in other words.

Example

MISUNDERSTANDING

sun, stand, standing, ding, dinged, miss, missed, under, understand, understanding, stand, standing, mist, misting, misted, and, mister, master, mastering, mast, team, meat, eat, tea, ate, stream, streaming, tear, dear, read, seam, under, mind, mine, miner, dine, diner, dime, sand, sanded, strand, stranded, dream, dune, dud, dude, dug, dig, drug, drag, red, star, stare, stared, art, tar, tare, rat, rate, rated, daring, sat, dare, sit, site, set, tis, seat, sing, sting, string, strung, strange, stair, mass, massed, mess, muster, mustard, staring, snare, snaring, stun, stunning, stunned, smear, smearing, same, sane, insane, said, game, dress, dressing, great, grate, nest, rest, gear, time, timed, timing, send, sending, dang, dart, darted, darting, guess, guest, gust, gusted, drain, rain, rained, grain, train, training, trained, main, stir, side, sided, siding, drum, tide, die, died, ride, guide, guided, grin, grinned, grand, gram, grade, graded, grant, grad, strain, strained, stain, stained, rude, smart, mud, mute, muted, darn, earn, during

References

Dr. Caroline Leaf, Switch On Your Brain, Baker Books, Baker Publishing Group, 2015.

Webster's II New Riverside University Dictionary, Houghton Mifflin Company, 1984.

You Go Words, internet search to find 12 to 20 letter words.

I also would like to acknowledge the activity department at the healthcare facility where I work for their dedication in helping the residents there to find words from words as an activity to help the residents keep moving forward. Participating with the activity staff is from where I found inspiration to work individually with persons to find words in other words.

About The Author

After experiencing a head injury in a head-on crash with a semi years ago, David has learned to enjoy stimulating his thought processes using word games and activities which help him to expand the way he thinks. Attempting to consider others as more important than himself, David shares words with others whenever possible to help them stimulate their thought processes as well and continue moving forward.

David read a book by Dr. Caroline Leaf called, Switch On Your Brain, in which she wrote, "Your brain is designed to respond to your mind." Also, "As we think, we change the physical nature of our brain. As we consciously direct our thinking, we can wire out toxic patterns of thinking and replace them with healthy thoughts. New thought networks grow. We increase our intelligence and bring healing to our brains, minds, and physical bodies."

David plans to continue finding words in other words as well as helping others switch on their brain with this practical exercise. He hopes that you will find this practice enjoyable and valuable also.

Made in the USA
Monee, IL
11 August 2021